THE BOGEYMAN

written by Steve Dover

illustrated by Alex Scahill

London | New York

Published by Clink Street Publishing 2020

Copyright © 2020

First edition.

The author asserts the moral right under the Copyright, Designs and Patents Act 1988 to be identified as the author of this work.

All rights reserved. No part of this publication may be reproduced, stored in a retrieval system or transmitted, in any form or by any means without the prior consent of the author, nor be otherwise circulated in any form of binding or cover other than that with which it is published and without a similar condition being imposed on the subsequent purchaser.

ISBN:
978-1-913568-85-6 - hardback
978-1-913568-65-8 - paperback
978-1-913568-66-5 - ebook

THE RAIN IT DRIP DROP DRIPS
FROM THE BRIM OF HIS DARK HAT,
AND BY HIS SIDE, HIS ONLY
FRIEND, A BLACK AND GHOSTLY CAT.

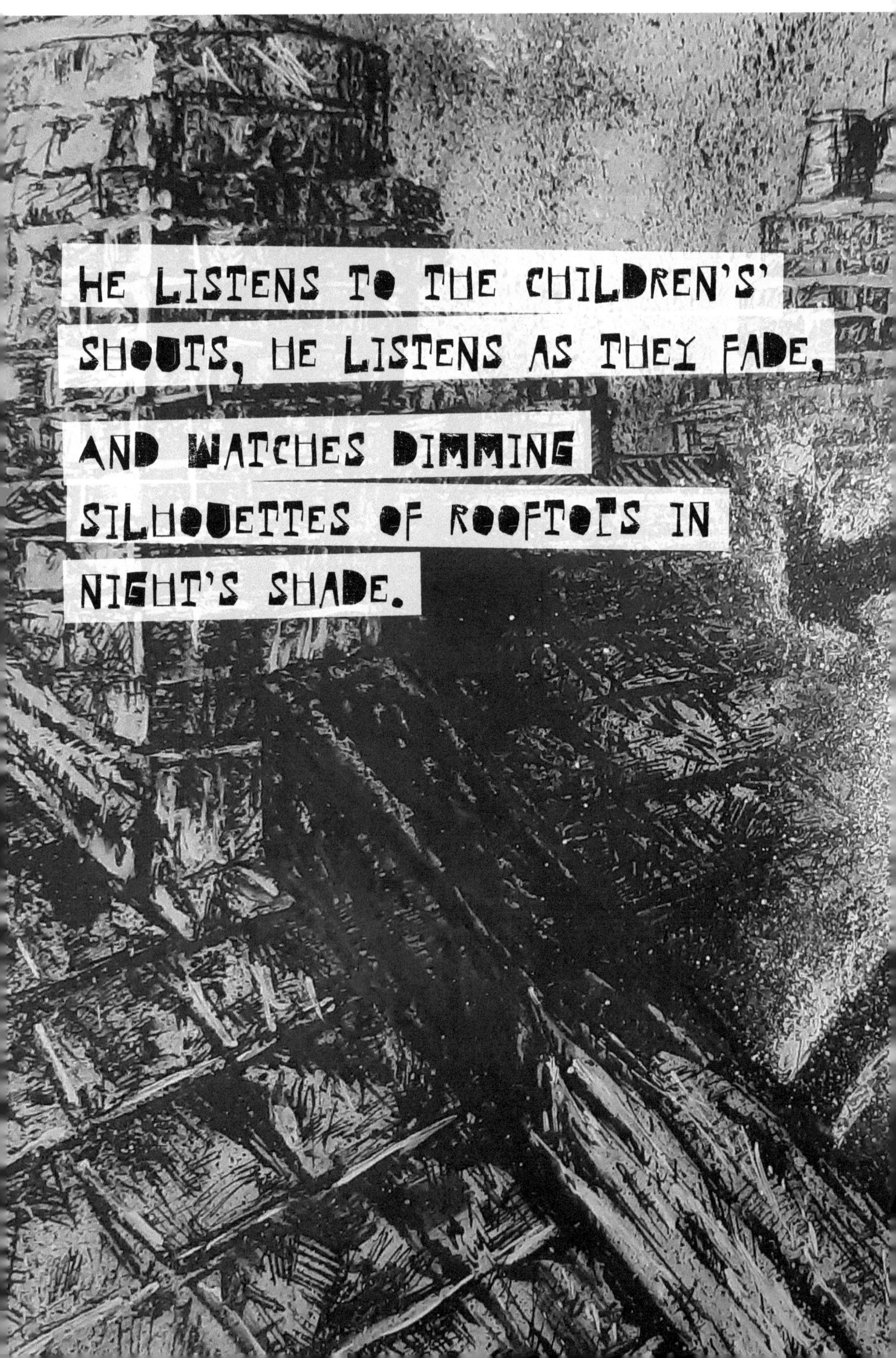

He listens to the children's' shouts, he listens as they fade, and watches dimming silhouettes of rooftops in night's shade.

He rises up and slinks along
and shins on down a drain,
then makes his lonely weary
way along the wet dark lane.

He frightens those who see him, but he really means no harm.
Long ago he fell beneath an evil witch's charm.

AND CHILDREN WITH YOU HE'D LIKE TO SING, YOUR GAMES HE'D LIKE TO PLAY

BUT SUNLIGHT HURTS HIS EYES SO MUCH AND HE'S BANISHED FROM THE DAY.

When at last the night is past
and dawn begins to rise,

is it a raindrop from his large
brimmed hat or a tear from
those sad eyes

that rolls to the end of
his long thin nose and drops
without a sound

to mingle with the other dew
that twinkles on the ground.

THE SUN SHE RISES HAZY AND TURNS THE MISTS TO GOLD, AND THE BOGEY MAN RETURNS TO HIS CATACOMBS DARK AND COLD.

AND ECHOING IN HIS DAILY DREAMS ARE SUNLIT DAYS OF JOY REMEMBERING SOME DISTANT TIME WHEN HE WAS JUST A BOY.

So next time you see the Bogey Man, don't run away in fear.

Remember that he'd like to dance and always have you near.

AND IF YOU SPY A HUDDLED FIGURE
LEANING ON YOUR CHIMNEY STACK
SPARE A THOUGHT FOR THE BOGEY
MAN WITH THE HUMP UPON HIS BACK.